AF578211

THE BATSFORD BOOK OF

THE POODLE

THE BATSFORD BOOK OF

THE POODLE

Harry Glover

B. T. BATSFORD LTD., LONDON

(frontispiece)
The sheer beauty of the poodle

First published 1974

ISBN 0 7134 2827 9

Filmset by Servis Filmsetting Ltd., Manchester
Printed and bound in Great Britain by
Wm. Clowes & Sons Ltd., London and Beccles
for the Publishers
B. T. BATSFORD LTD.
4 Fitzhardinge Street, London W1H 0AH

Contents

Acknowledgments

The Author and Publishers wish to thank the following for permission to reproduce the photographs appearing in this book:

Animal Photography Ltd and Sally Anne Thompson for pages 15, 16, 19, 22, 23, 24, 25, 27, 28, 29, 32, 33, 35, 36, 41, 43, 44, 45, 46, 48, 49, 50, 52, 53, 55, 57, 60, 61, 63, 68, 69, 70, 72, 77, 80, 83, 84, 89, 90, 91 and 93

Barratts for page 39

Camera Clix for page 76

Colour Library International for pages 11, 20, 21 and 73

Croydon Advertiser for pages 35 and 84

Anne Cumbers for pages 14, 18, 26, 34, 65, 71, 74 and 88

Evening News for pages 2, 51, 54, 58 and 75

Thomas Fall for pages 31 and 40

Fox Photos for pages 78 and 87

Alan Fulwood for page 79

William P. Gilbert for page 86

Dagmar Kenis for page 85

Kirrans Kennels for page 75

Diane Pearce for pages 42 and 59

Varitonia Poodles for pages 62 and 82

Introduction

Most of the breeds of dog known to man can be placed into one or another group by type, the work that they do, or by their characteristics. Since they have been domesticated for centuries, these characteristics are the different ways in which they react to man. Spaniels are notoriously the sentimentalists, terriers are by tradition the trouble-makers, some are faithful, some independent. If the poodle is to be classified in this way, then it must be as the entertainer.

Quite apart from their long association with the stage and the circus (for they can be trained to do almost anything), poodles are by nature the most entertaining dogs that we know. They are gay, assertive, buoyant, and complete extroverts. If there is mischief afoot they are bound to be mixed up with it; if the day is to be a quiet one they will entertain themselves, but if it is to be fun and games then they will be the first to join in.

When they greet you after your return from even a short trip away, they leave no doubt that they are hysterically delighted. They express themselves with their voice, their expression, even with their whole body, laughing and barking, jumping head high if they are large enough and young enough, making it quite clear that they are greeting you, not as their master, but as one of them. Their physical structure is such that they can stand on two legs almost as easily as on four, and in their competition to attract attention they will dance round like a collection of puppets on strings.

They become attached to people, but will switch allegiance from one person to another more freely than will most dogs. If the one person in the household that has been their particular friend is away from home, they don't pine, they just turn to someone else, and while they are most companionable, their attachment can be to anyone in the family group. For they are so intelligent that they seem to understand the human family system, and want to join it as a full member.

They are more friendly with one another than most other breeds. They are not inclined to fight, and quarrelling is very much more a matter of noise than of real violence. While with some breeds keeping a number together presents problems, often leading to tremendous battles, serious injuries and even fatalities, poodles that are kept together seem to develop a 'pecking order', with a dominant male or female that keeps order among the young ones. For this reason it is possible, even advisable, to keep more than one, as they will usually live, eat and sleep together in complete harmony.

They are easily trained, and are often seen in competition with Alsatians and border collies in the obedience rings at our shows, performing feats of obedience and intelligence that many breeds cannot even attempt. Add to this the fact that they have handsome good looks, a coat that repays constant attention, and that they come in various sizes and many delightful colours and you have a breed with the sort of appeal that has taken them rapidly to a very high position in the popularity poll.

History of the Breed

The history of the poodle is complicated by the fact that they were for so long called the French Poodle. But although they have been known in France for a long time, and although it was the artists of the French stage and circus who first realised and exploited their potential as performing dogs, they almost certainly originated in Germany.

It is never wise to be dogmatic about the origin of any breed of dog, but it

The original Water Dog

is almost certain that the poodle began life as the early Water Dog or Pudel of Germany. The similarity, seen so clearly if one compares the engraving of 1803 of the Water Dog with the photographs of the mismarked black and white poodles, while not proof of a relationship, is at least evidence. The Water Dog looked like a black and white poodle with a short face and a neglected coat.

The stories of the intelligence of the Water Dogs, the way in which they could be trained and their general response to education, sound so much like

German Poodles from a nineteenth-century engraving

the poodle as it was known during the last century. There is a hint, too, in some of the old books on the subject, that there existed in early days a refined form of Water Dog 'with elegant form more calculated to please for domestic and social purposes'. 'The Water Dog even in puppyhood displays an eager desire to be employed in offices of domestic amusement.' This sounds just like a poodle. A later quote reads: 'the Water Dog or Poodle of the Germans is, in its most perfect state, not a British race, but rose in favour first in Germany, and during the revolutionary wars was carried by the troops into France, and only in the later campaigns became familiar to the British in Spain and the Netherlands. No dog is more intelligent or attached to his master; none like a poodle can trace out and find lost property with more certainty and perseverance.'

Another admirer of the breed wrote: 'in Germany and indeed throughout the whole of Northern Europe he (the poodle) is looked upon as every whit as useful a companion as he is ornamental, and the appearance of a poodle harnessed to a cart or carrying his master's basket is a very common one in the streets of Germany, Holland and Belgium.'

There is little doubt that poodles were first bred in Germany. The name in the German language is Pudel, and dogs that were so close in appearance to the poodle as we know it today that they could hardly be anything else, appear in engravings of the sixteenth century – in, for instance, the family group of Maximillian of Austria and de Vos's painting of Tobit and his dog.

They spread both East and West. In Russia they became large and black, lithe and agile. In central Germany they became heavier and stronger, in Belgium they were massive and pulled milk carts whilst in France smaller ones called Barbets that were essentially toy dogs or companions were developed. Many other breeds were probably connected with poodles in the early days, such as the Sheep Poodle of Germany which could well have been the Komodor that we know today; though recently emanating from Hungary, it is large, poodle-like, and essentially a herding dog. Even the Little Lion Dog, that comes from either Russia or Malta (depending upon which authority one follows!), could have been closely related in the early days.

In addition there was the difference in coat, from the coarse wiry coat of the early Russian type to the corded poodle coat that was at one time so popular but which has now gone out of favour.

It was suggested before the turn of the century that the mere division of

A corded poodle of the late nineteenth century

the breed by size was not a good thing. But this is exactly what in fact has happened, and poodles are now divided into Standard Poodles, the big ones, those that were probably originally the large gundogs of the continent; the Miniatures, those that have been for so long the most popular ones at our shows; and Toy Poodles, the small ones that were kept entirely as companions, the Barbets of France, those that have now almost overhauled the Miniatures in the Show World.

From Canis Familiaris Aquaticus – the original Water Dog – to the present-day Poodle is, historically, quite a long way. But even if the appearance has changed radically, the character, intelligence and wit have remained.

Puppies

Like all animals, poodles begin life as babies, needing all the care and attention to warmth, feeding, and general wellbeing, that a human baby needs. But whereas one cannot normally choose a human baby, one can look at a whole number of poodles before choosing the one that is going to spend the next ten years or so with you as its companion. So it will be as well to say something about choosing a puppy.

Having decided on size and colour – and unless one is going to become a very serious breeder of poodles those are the only two decisions that need making – the next thing to decide is where the puppy is to come from. Here it is necessary to do a certain amount of study. There are shops, dealers, breeders and kennels, and the decision as to which one is likely to be the best depends on so many considerations. Good puppies can be found in shops, having often been unloaded by someone who enthusiastically decided to breed a litter of puppies and then discovered that they could not be managed, but this is probably the exception rather than the rule. The shop is not always the best place to buy a puppy.

Nor for the same reason is a dealer's a good place to buy a puppy as the dealer is not usually interested in where puppies came from, their parentage, and whether they are good stock or not. The best place is almost certainly

A nest full of babies

A Standard Poodle mother somewhat bored with everything

The smallest puppy and the largest poodle

the kennels run by a serious breeder of poodles, the sort of place that has a fairly large number of dogs, does quite a lot of showing, and has made a reputation both showing dogs and breeding them. This sort of person cannot afford to risk having a reputation injured by supplying a puppy that is not worth the money demanded, so that he will usually give a good deal.

One of the problems with poodles is that few, if any, breeders breed regularly from all three sizes and the various colours of poodles, so that to get what you want you may have to travel some distance. You may well ask why it is that if you only want a poodle as a pet you should go to all the trouble of seeking out someone who is definitely breeding high-class stock for the show ring, and the answer is just that – that it is high-class stock.

Since the number of poodles bred has increased at an incredible rate in recent years and sales have been easy there has been a tendency for standards to fall. Only the dedicated breeder makes sure that, in breeding dogs that will do well in the showring, only the very best parents are selected and only the best possible puppies are bred. If you are going to have a poodle, then you might just as well have a good one. You will be more proud of it; you will not be disappointed when you see it alongside other dogs. The breeder will have been just as careful in breeding for intelligence and character as he has been for good looks, and your chances of getting a dog that will turn out to be

Poodles are quite happy with anyone's puppies

They like company

obedient and worthwhile as a companion are increased by buying from someone with a reputation for good dogs.

In order to find out where such a puppy can be bought you will need to make contact with breeders through reading the specialist magazines and journals. These contain advertisements for all the best kennels with puppies for sale. If in addition you can get the advice of an expert in your locality, not necessarily a poodle person, this would be helpful. He or she would be able to tell you about people who have poodles that they have met at shows, or who they know have puppies, and you can save yourself a good deal of time and trouble by seeking this sort of advice.

(opposite)
An apricot poodle puppy surveying the world

Having discovered the whereabouts of poodle puppies of the size and colour that you require, the next thing is to go to see them to make your

Poodles and cats get on well together

NOT TESSA!!

choice. If you can get your local dog expert to go with you and help, this would be ideal, as you are looking for points with which you are probably not familiar. The puppy which appeals most to you, and the one that unaided you would probably choose, has perhaps got something wrong with it that you cannot see, and others which have nothing wrong and which you have overlooked would almost certainly be better for you.

Poodle puppies looking for something to play with

(overleaf) Two little apricot poodles looking bewildered

When choosing a puppy it is almost as important to see the parents, or at least the mother, as it is to see the puppies. You can tell a good deal about how the puppies have been reared by looking at her as well as the babies. Both she and they should be clean and fresh looking, well fed, with clean and shiny coats, and housed in a clean warm place with plenty of bedding and water.

Then you will need to decide whether you want a female, with the problems that this presents as well as the delights of better companionship which they undoubtedly have, or a male, free from the trouble of breeding, but generally more independent, and even at times less trustworthy.

Having settled all this, you must make your choice. Choose a puppy that is healthy with clear eyes and an alert expression, interested in everything that is going on, inquisitive to the point of being mischievous, and one that in the rough and tumble of the pen is holding its own and not allowing itself to be bullied. This is not a clear-cut decision, as the one that sits back

A puppy of four-and-a-half months partly trimmed

and watches the others at play could be equally good temperamentally, but just reserved. So long as he is taking an interest in what is going on, and is not looking cowed, he may be just the one.

One of the best ways of setting about buying a puppy is to go to a number of shows, see the dogs, and talk to the exhibitors. In this way you will pick up a great deal of useful information, and may at the same time learn of someone who has just the puppy that you are looking for.

Finally, don't look for bargains. Puppies are very expensive to produce and rear. The housing and feeding of the mother for a year prior to her having the litter is in itself a great deal of trouble and expense and poodles do not have large litters. If a breeder has kept the mother for twelve months, paid a stud fee, the vet, and all the special feed, and the final result is three puppies, it is hardly likely that the puppies will be available at bargain prices. You will generally get what you pay for, and in just the same way as you would hardly expect to get a Rolls Royce for the price of a Mini, you cannot expect to get a show champion for the price of a pet.

(preceding page) A very sedate baby puppy

Rearing a Puppy

The usual age at which a puppy will leave its mother is eight weeks. At this age it will still be thinking of milk as its natural food and its mother's warmth as its natural surroundings. It will certainly have been introduced to solid food (the breeder will have seen to that), but the change from the nest to the outside world is a big one, and can be quite a shock. Remember that everything changes suddenly – the people, the noises, the shapes and sizes of objects, the temperature and the food. Try to see these changes from the puppy's point of view, and make sure that you do everything to make the transition from the old surroundings to the new as easy as possible.

(overleaf)
Having a friend helps

Most breeders supply diet sheets with the puppies, some even provide a small quantity of the food to which the puppy has been accustomed, in order to tide you over this difficult period. It is then up to you to do all that you

A Miniature Poodle with five puppies

(preceding page)
A family group

can to see that the puppy's life at this stage is made as easy and comfortable as possible. You are now on your own.

Although nothing can take the place of experience when dealing with the problems surrounding the rearing of a puppy, a good book on the subject is the next best thing. Many of the firms who supply dog foods do in fact provide owners with a good deal of excellent information about how to feed dogs from puppyhood to old age. Moreover, with the modern methods of producing dog foods, feeding is extremely simple.

One of the primary requirements of a puppy is a warm, sheltered place in which to sleep. Puppies at an early age spend most of their time eating, playing and sleeping (roughly in that order), so you must provide the right sort of place in which the puppy can play and sleep. He will, from birth, have been accustomed to a warm and fairly dark place in which to sleep, so he should be provided with a basket or box lined with something sanitary and comfortable, and placed in a warm spot away from draughts.

If you keep him in the house, his exercise and play will be your responsibility. Rooms with carpets are not ideal, and accidents will happen that will

A bit lonely

Quite grown up

make the puppy unpopular. It is therefore a good idea to arrange exercise for the puppy immediately after food, preferably out of doors, and failing that in an enclosed place under cover. Remember he needs help with his play. A puppy needs toys just as much as a child does. It is no use enclosing a young puppy in a bare area with nothing for him to pull about and chase; he must have toys. Not woolly bears and celluloid ducks, but pieces of strong hard material that he can tow around or throw about, chew and generally work off his energies upon until he is tired. He will then need to retire to his comfortable, quiet, darkened bed in the box or basket.

If a routine of this sort is followed, the puppy will lead a healthy life and a happy one. He will very quickly become only attached to his surroundings, and the problem of house training will rapidly disappear. Poodles are intelligent and naturally anxious to please, and training of the puppy can begin immediately. Not making him jump through a hoop, but just the simple training: when to be quiet and when to play, which things are his and

(overleaf)
When groomed for show they look beautiful

(preceding page)
Showing the long well-cared-for ears

which things he must leave alone, and the simple matter of obeying a few essential commands.

It is essential that, whatever you decide to train your puppy to do, you display endless patience and complete insistence at all times. Dogs are creatures of habit, and the right habits – such as remaining quiet except when noise is needed, travelling quietly in the car, going to bed when it is required, guarding and yet at the same time accepting visitors who have a right to be there – these can all be inculcated by constant training at a receptive age. If the training is neglected until the dog is too old, or not carried out consistently and constantly, a spoiled dog will result, one that is a nuisance to everyone – owners, visitors and neighbours alike. An obedient dog is a happy dog.

In order that your poodle shall be able to enjoy a walk, it is essential that he should be lead-trained. Most puppies object to a lead at first, and if you attempt to put on a collar and take the puppy out for a walk right away, you will have trouble and neither you nor the puppy will enjoy it. First of all put a light collar on the puppy and leave it there for some days until he has grown accustomed to it. Only then introduce the restraint of a lead, and initially don't attempt to tow the puppy round with it. For a while the puppy will object and probably want to go in every direction but the one that you wish to take. For a while let him do this until he has grown used to the idea that, if he comes in the same direction as you, then you can both be together all the time. With patience you will find that in a remarkably short time the puppy is following you, and the lead is incidental.

The lead and collar can then be abandoned as an everyday piece of equipment. The dog will quickly learn that the production of them means a walk, and will look forward eagerly to the whole routine of collar and lead being produced, the collar being put on and then going out for a walk.

It would be remarkable if a puppy could be reared to adulthood without some trouble in the way of illness or the suspicion of illness. It is therefore a good idea to have him checked a couple of times by your veterinary surgeon even though there is nothing wrong with him. This can be done at least once when the puppy is inoculated at around twelve weeks, but another check or two while the puppy is growing is advisable. In any event at the slightest suspicion of illness you shall take your dog to the vet. It may be nothing, but it could be serious.

The Entertainer

The poodle is a natural entertainer. He is born with a desire to please, and possesses a friendly and extrovert character. With his natural tendency to stand on his hindlegs and dance around, the poodle displays a near-human quality that has been exploited by man.

The earliest record of a poodle that appeared to have gifts beyond those of the normal dog, is that of a dog named Boy which was brought back to England by Prince Rupert, after he had been held prisoner in Europe and came back to help Charles I fight against the Roundheads. He is said to have had the powers of speech in several languages, and died at the battle of Marston Moor in 1644.

The Prince Regent who became George IV had a poodle that was his constant companion, and in more recent years Sir Winston Churchill had a pet poodle called Rufus. So poodles have for centuries occupied high places as friends of the famous, both as companions and entertainers, for men

Simple tricks are easy for poodles

Even the older ones love a game

who had the cares of affairs of state would need diversion as well as companionship.

As early as the eighteenth century there were performing poodles in England. One particular troupe of dogs gave a performance before Royalty which included dancing and eating at table. They did all the circus turns that were more normally performed by human acrobats, walking tightropes, balancing on front as well as hind legs, opening and shutting cupboards, and even carrying out the counting trick barking the correct number of times to a displayed card.

Poodles were developed as entertainers in France during the last century, where showmen trained them to perform a great variety of tricks, whether in the streets, in the circus or on stage. Even to this day there is one illusionist who instead of producing a dove from a silk handkerchief produces a Toy Poodle. He performs with an orchestra and the poodle sits on top of the piano and in his own fashion sings while the band plays.

(opposite)
They will pose almost anywhere

Although clowns probably originated in Italy, they became a very important part of the entertainment at French circuses and on the French stage.

They will play with anything or anyone

As circus artists they are supreme

(below right)
They stand on their hind legs quite naturally when greeting

(below)
They stand without support for fun

The early French clowns often used performing poodles as part of their act, and it has been said that the bands of long hair left on the legs of poodles originated from the attempt to make the performing poodle match the pompoms that were traditionally worn by the clowns. It is, however, much more likely that they were in fact left on to protect and keep warm the vulnerable joints of the poodles' legs when they were being used as gundogs and entering water after game.

There are endless tales of the intelligence and faithfulness of poodles,

(opposite)
Later standing can become a performance

such as the famous poodle of the Pont Neuf who dirtied the boots of passers-by so that his master, a shoeblack who had his stall on the bridge, would have a guarantee of continued good trade. Munito, in 1818 kept Paris entertained with his command of arithmetic and card tricks. There is even a tale of a white poodle that committed suicide.

Poodles have also been used in war, like the famous Moustache, who in the early nineteenth century was on the strength of the French Grenadiers. He went through several campaigns with them, including Marengo and Austerlitz, and is even said to have rescued the regimental colours when the grenadier carrying them was killed in action. He was killed at the battle of Badajoz in 1811 and was buried on the field of battle complete with collar and medal.

It is usually the more excitable puppy that will be the most easily trained to perform tricks. The one that rushes to greet a friend, that bounces around, making noises and wagging its tail, this will be the one that will eventually turn out to be the best performer. Poodles love doing tricks, and it is noticeable that in any performance by poodles, whether it be in the circus ring, on stage, or even in the home, their tails are wagging all the time. They clearly enjoy performing and entertaining people. For them the whole of life is a game to be enjoyed to the full all the time.

Some people misguidedly argue that it is cruel to train dogs to perform

It starts at an early age whilst playing

Dim

Poodles are quite happy fooling around

tricks and feats of intelligence and memory. They claim that dogs do not naturally jump through hoops and run around on their hind legs. But in the case of poodles, who enjoy doing all these things so much, to whom jumping and running around is play, to deny them would be in fact cruel.

They like playacting

Anyone who has watched the obedience classes at a big dog show will have seen how even the much more sedate breeds, such as golden retrievers and labradors, express their genuine pleasure at an exercise well performed. Poodles, who are much more responsive, enjoy every minute of it to the full.

The Coat of the Poodle

There is no other breed that has in recent years increased in popularity as fast as poodles. This is shown, not only by the large numbers that are seen around in homes and streets as pets, but in the numbers that are registered each year at the Kennel Club.

One of the factors that has brought about this enormous increase in popularity is the sheer beauty of the breed, as depicted on cards and calendars

Champion Sunshine

Beautifully prepared

by professional photographers. It is only when someone has owned a poodle that they can appreciate the breed for its character, but they are almost certainly influenced in their original choice by the wonderful photographs they have seen. Poodles are remarkably photogenic, as will be seen from the plates shown in this book, and a good deal of this quality is due to the fact

A very proud Mista Softee

that the coat is not only beautiful in itself, but that it repays attention so well. There are few sights more striking in the animal world than a poodle with its coat groomed to perfection, with every hair in place, and showing the delightful shapes that can be produced by the expert trimmer.

Interest in poodles as show dogs was first evinced in the latter part of the nineteenth century, the Poodle Club of Great Britain being formed in 1876 and given recognition in 1896. At that time there was a considerable amount of traffic between countries in show poodles, dogs crossing from England to America and in the reverse direction. Dogs were imported from Germany and France, and almost all the poodles concerned were of what was called the corded variety.

The coats of the corded poodles were allowed to grow, and were never combed out. They were kept soaked in oil and wrapped up to prevent them from becoming damaged. The result was that the coat fell into tight curls which grew longer and tighter as time went by, with great competition developing as to which dog had the longest and tightest cords. It was said that in some countries the coat was loaded with butter and the dogs stood near to a fire when the fat needed removing; whereupon it all melted and dripped out. One of the problems with the early corded poodles was that they were not allowed to be shown with any grease remaining in the coat.

Head study of a white champion

The task of bathing a greased-up corded poodle was such that few were actually shown.

At the turn of the century the Kennel Club in England decided to divide poodles into corded and curly and the curly ones gradually took over. Up to the beginning of the First World War almost all the poodles shown were what we now would call Standards in that they were large, and the majority of them were of the corded variety. Attempts had been made to have the length of the cords on this variety limited, so that they should not drag on the ground. An approach was made to the Kennel Club in an attempt to get permission for the corded poodles to be shown with the oil remaining in their coats, but it was to no avail, and the curly poodles with their much easier preparation, gradually superseded them.

This opened the way for the poodle to become a popular breed. Its quaint merry character, its wholehearted enthusiasm for everything and its ability to fit in with a household, was already endearing it to many people. Only the coat difficulty had held it back.

The great difference between the coat of a poodle and that of any other breed is the fact that not only is clipping permitted for show, which makes it unique, but that it is encouraged for all poodles, even those that are kept purely as pets. Some people represent the clipping and trimming of poodles

Care and attention pays

The most popular show colour is black

as a great difficulty and one of the reasons why they are a nuisance, but this is not so. There is a great deal of pleasure in trimming a poodle so that it looks its best, as well as the joy of creation, for the well-trimmed poodle is really quite an art form.

There is satisfaction too in the fact that the clipping of poodles has a long tradition behind it. It is not just a modern fashion or a whim of the dog show fraternity. Poodles have been clipped for centuries, as can be seen from old paintings which show poodles clipped in the Lion Clip; in trimming a poodle we are thus continuing a tradition that has been almost worldwide.

The removing of the long hair from the hind end of poodles was almost certainly in order that they should not be hindered in their work as water dogs. They were used in Europe, particularly to retrieve game falling in water. But anyone who has seen an unshorn sheep in water will know how a

Head of a black best-in-show winner

wealth of coat can be a severe hindrance in deep water. Tufts of hair were left round the bone joints to protect those joints from the cold and wet of the water. For it is surprising how long hair will protect the skin and prevent water from getting to it. If you part the hair of a long-coated dog that has been for a swim and appears completely soaked, you will find that unless he has been in the water for a long time, the skin underneath will be remarkably dry. It was this that persuaded the early poodle keepers to let the hair on the joints grow long while the remainder was clipped.

The accepted forms that the clipping of poodles takes are Lion Clip, Dutch Clip, Lamb Trim, Continental Clip and Puppy Clip. The only features that are common to all forms are the feet, face and tail, all of which are trimmed to the shorter coat. The Lion Clip is the one most extensively used, and the only one that is recommended for the show poodle – except in the case of puppies that are expected to remain in Puppy Clip until the coat has grown sufficiently for the Lion Clip to be worthwhile.

The clipping of poodles into these patterns has been the subject of a good deal of misguided ridicule. The uninformed see it as pandering to fashion, and do not understand that clipping is not only a tradition but vital to the wellbeing of the dog. A poodle with all its hair allowed to grow would be overheated and unhealthy, impossible to keep clean and free from tangles, and a ready host to all sorts of vermin.

Anyone who intends clipping their own poodle should go to the trouble of getting some instruction in the art. It is possible to get this from books, many of which contain diagrams explaining how each style of clip is arrived at, the steps to take, and how the clip is maintained, but no book learning can take the place of some practical training. Unfortunately this is not as easy as it sounds, as the clipping of poodles has become big business and there are few sizeable towns that do not have at least one Poodle Parlour. Naturally those who run this type of establishment are hardly likely to pass on their secrets.

There are, however, breeders and exhibitors of poodles who are far too busy with their own dogs to bother with clipping professionally and who would be kind enough to show a beginner how the job is done. Fortunately the effects of clipping are not irrevocable; the hair of the poodle grows continually, and even if at first the beginner's efforts are not perfect, time will remove the blemishes, and the clipper will improve with practice.

(opposite)
Show posing they love

With a pair of clippers, both hand and electric, some round-nose scissors, a brush and a comb, anyone can have a great deal of enjoyment trying to get the best out of their poodle. In order to enjoy the exercise to the full, the cooperation of the poodle is essential, and here is where the extreme tractability of poodles shows. They can be trained to stand and to lie still not only accepting the inevitable, but even enjoying the fuss that goes with it. Young puppies will often object, but with the firm and consistent handling that is part of basic puppy training, they soon grow to enjoy it.

But the basic part of looking after your puppy's coat is grooming; the more exacting experience of clipping, that comes later. Puppies need to be groomed daily from the age of about eight weeks, being made to lie down on their side on a table, and having the coat sorted out and brushed right down to the skin.

Head study showing the show preparation of ears and topknot

Every hair in place

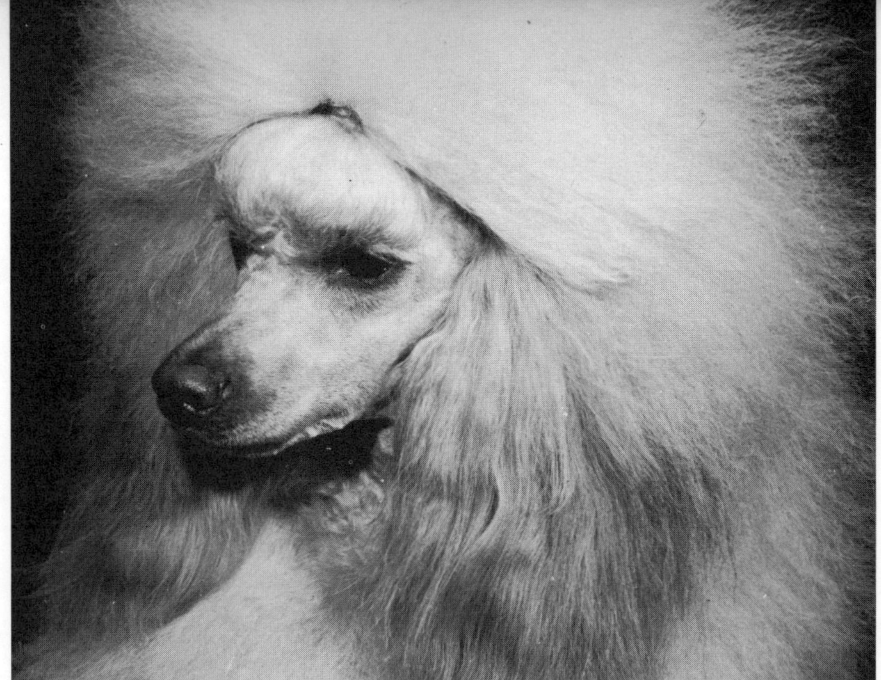

In this way tangles will be avoided, and the later work of clipping and bathing will be made much easier.

It is important that the puppy should understand from a very early age that the process of grooming is not a game, and he should be prevented from playing with the tools or joining in the process. Eventually it will become so enjoyable an experience that poodles spend most of their time on the grooming table, sleeping or dozing while the grooming goes on.

Fortunately for the poodle owner, bathing poodles does the coat no harm providing that the correct form of shampoo is used. There are many successful shampoos on the market that are recommended for poodles and one of these should be used. Unclean dogs are smelly dogs, which is why it is fortunate that the poodles can be frequently bathed. As they are more often than not kept in the house as family pets, it is essential that they should be kept clean and free from odour.

Drying them is no problem. Some people use electric hair-dryers; some, when the weather is warm enough, dry them out of doors.

It all sounds like a good deal of work, but it is rewarding work, and the finished effect, drawing admiring comments from anyone who sees the finished article, makes it all worth while.

Size in Poodles

Originally all poodles of whatever size were registered just as poodles. This meant that any dog resembling a poodle, whether the size of a terrier or a collie, would be classed as a poodle. This led to confusion, as other breeds were standardised by size, and everyone knew roughly what to expect.

In Europe, particularly in the Netherlands, poodles were bred large enough to pull small carts and help with delivering goods. At the same time small ones were kept as pets and in France this breed was known as le Petit Barbet. Then there were Great Poodles, Middle Poodles and Little Poodles all lumped together. Something had to be done to avoid the complete confusion that would result from mixed breeding.

In 1911 the Kennel Club decided that the smaller poodles should be registered as a separate variety, to measure under 15 inches at the shoulder, and so the Miniature Poodle was born. It was many years later and after a long battle for recognition that the Toy Poodle came into being, not in fact

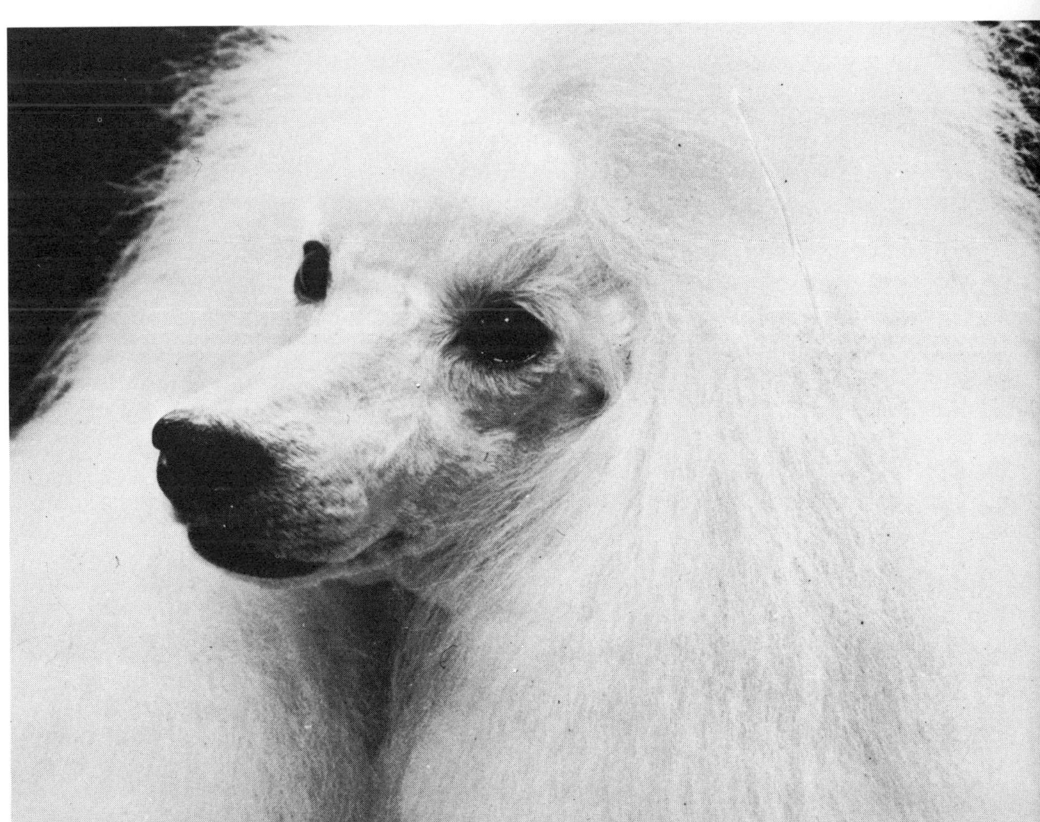

The dark eyes and nose of Cleopatra

(overleaf) An apricot Toy Poodle

(preceding page)
A delightful head study of a Toy Poodle

until 1957. In Britain the maximum height was fixed at 11 inches, in the USA 10 inches. These regulations were until very recently most rigidly enforced, the standard reading that they 'must' be under the respective height limit for the variety.

While we still have poodles of all sizes (such as Toys that are just over the limit or Standards that are just over the limit of height for Miniatures) we

Champion Cleopatra and her daughter

A young black poodle

do now have three separate breeds, distinguished one from the other by height. One interesting fact is that, although they are all very different in size, they all have the same standard, and are not distinguished in any other way.

Temperamentally there is little to choose between the three sizes. Since they all come from the same root stock it might be expected that all poodles would be identical in temperament. In fact it does not quite work out that way, as Toys tend to be the most affectionate, Miniatures the most lively, and Standards the steadiest. As always, there will be exceptions, but generally this will hold good.

(overleaf)
Silver Toy champion from Sweden

Colour in Poodles

(preceding page)
A windblown hairdo

One nearly asleep is guarded by the other

According to the standard any single solid colour is acceptable in poodles. White markings are a fault, and the clearer the colour the better. A white poodle must be a pure white and must not have any cream or lemon markings.

The popular colours are black, white, silver and apricot, with rather fewer browns and blues, and these clear self-colours have been arrived at by

(overleaf)
In repose

careful selective breeding. At one time poodles came in a mixture of colours, even light liver or dark grey with black patches.

Parti-coloured poodles were often bred in the past, and from time to time still appear. Today they are not permissible for show, which is perhaps a pity as they can be most decorative. There is an early description of a white poodle with black pompoms on the back and tail, and many of the early poodles depicted in paintings were of mixed colours.

This search for pure colour often led to the using of colouring matter to correct dubious marks or tendencies towards another colour, a practice which led to the term 'poodle faking'. Any form of colouring matter is now completely barred for dogs that are shown. At one time however it was quite popular for a woman to have her poodle's coat dyed to match her hair or outfit: one might see a fashionable lady with blue-rinsed hair walking the street with a blue-rinsed poodle, or one in a pink dress with her poodle dyed to match.

Apart from the blacks, poodles change colour from puppyhood, only

A fine Standard Poodle, Royal Sovereign

A champion black Standard Poodle

(preceding page) Head of a Standard Poodle

getting their true colour as they grow their mature coat. It is therefore often difficult to tell exactly what colour a puppy will turn out to be when it is mature. Apricot puppies are much darker than apricot adults, blue puppies look black when they are born, and the silvers look so dark when they are born that they could almost be blacks.

It is as well when buying a puppy to have a good look at both of the parents

Looking down his nose

(overleaf)
A gorgeous white Standard Poodle in full coat

if possible to make sure that they are of the colour you want, and preferably that they are both the same colour. From time to time breeders introduce a mixture of colour to improve pigmentation or to darken eyes and noses, and this can be dangerous unless the breeder knows exactly what he is doing.

Colour seems to be linked with temperament, probably due to the ancestry and the various lines that produced the different colours. Whites are said

A lovely black Standard Poodle

to be more placid; certainly they were considered preferable for training by the early circus people, who always preferred them for this reason. Blacks and browns are more energetic, and silvers tend to be more highly strung. These are debatable points, but certain breeders believe that there is a connection between colour and temperament.

In some countries slight variations in colour are accepted, such as white markings, changes of colour on the longer hairs and a certain amount of shading; but in Britain any of these would be taken into account in the showring. For pets, it matters not at all what colours poodles are, and not all breeders destroy puppies that are mismarked. The potential pet owner thus has the opportunity of acquiring, inexpensively, a perfectly good and indeed very lovely poodle and one that has the added attraction of being different from anyone else's.

(preceding page) Winning best in show at Windsor

Showing a Poodle

Having read so far and having looked at the photographs, you may well decide to buy a poodle, may even have bought one, and you now want to show it.

The first thing to do is to get all the paperwork completed. There is nothing more disappointing or embarrassing than to go to a show and find that the necessary forms have not been correctly completed, with the result that your dog can either not be shown, or appears in someone else's name.

Probably one of the greatest Standards, Champion Tall Dark and Handsome

(overleaf) Looking just as well at home

(preceding page)
A silver Miniature in Pet Clip

Tall Dark and Handsome having a bath

If you have bought your poodle from any good kennel and have indicated that you might eventually wish to show it, you will probably find that it is already registered. Most of the big kennels register their puppies before selling them, so that your dog will already have a registered name at the Kennel Club. However, you still want it to be in your name, so you need to carry out the process known as transferring. This entails obtaining a form of

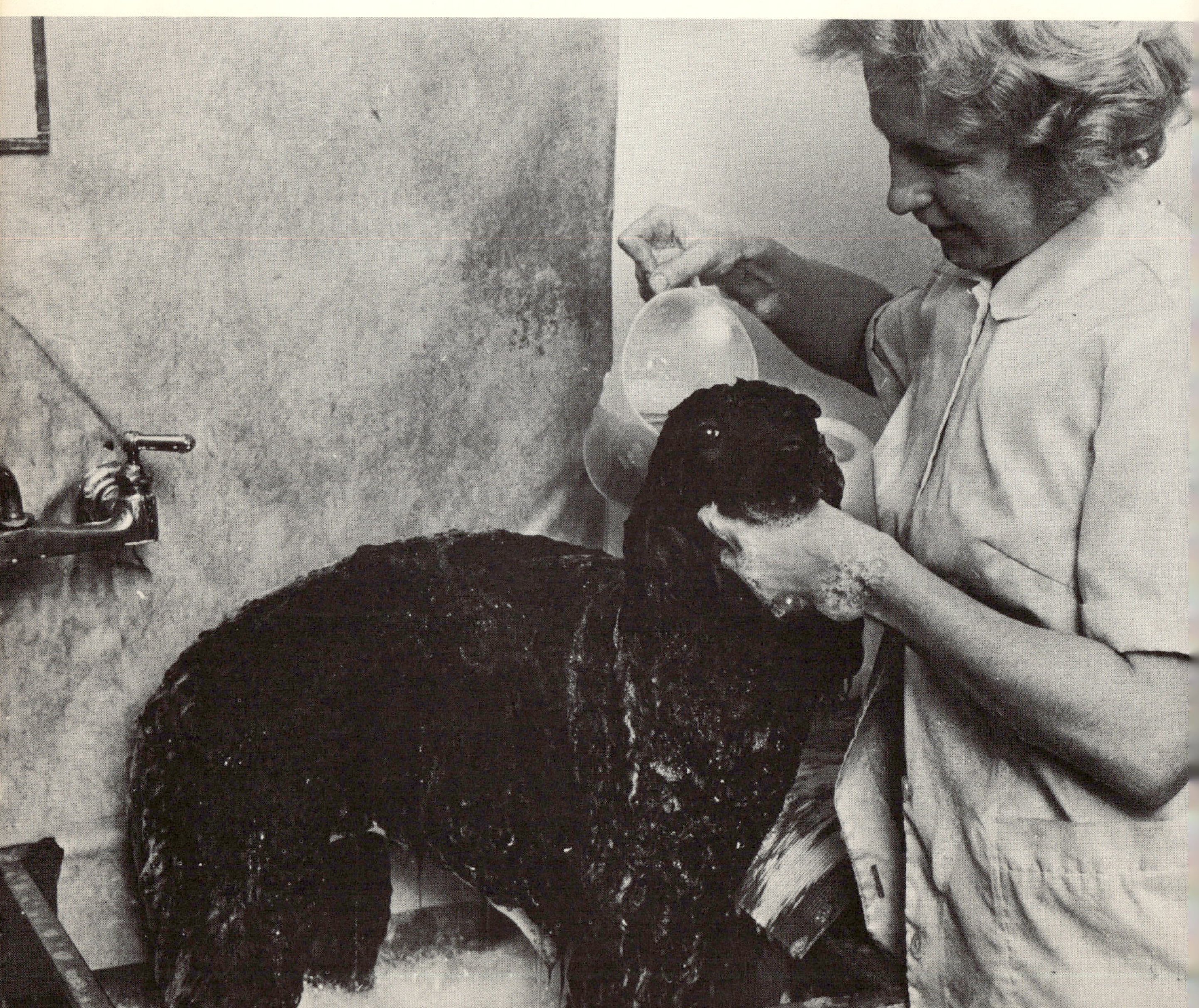

Getting ready for a show

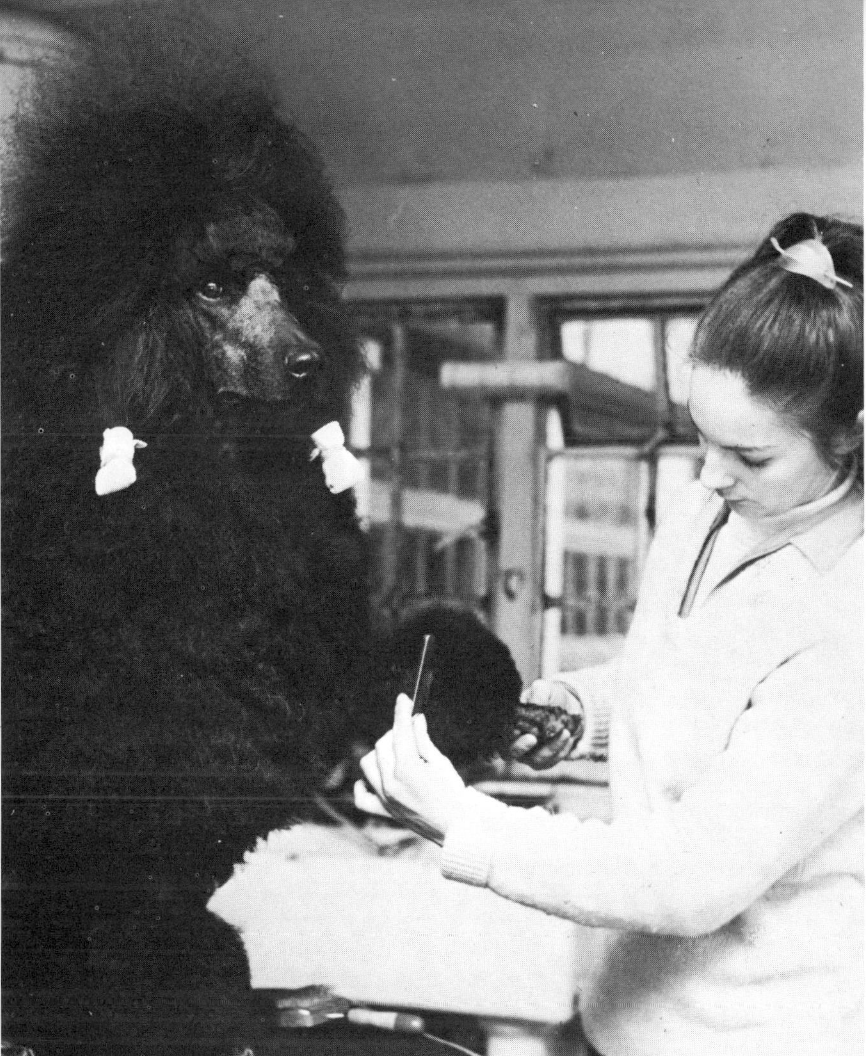

transfer either from the breeder, who will usually carry a stock, or from the Kennel Club. This will need signing by the breeder and by you, and must then be sent to the Kennel Club together with a small fee. You cannot change the name of the dog (it is his for life) but there is nothing to stop you from giving a pet name which can be used everywhere except at a show. Once all this has been done, you can show your dog when he has reached the age of six months.

(Overleaf)
Head of a silver poodle

One of the first things that you should do is to join your nearest breed club.

(preceding page)
A white Pet Poodle

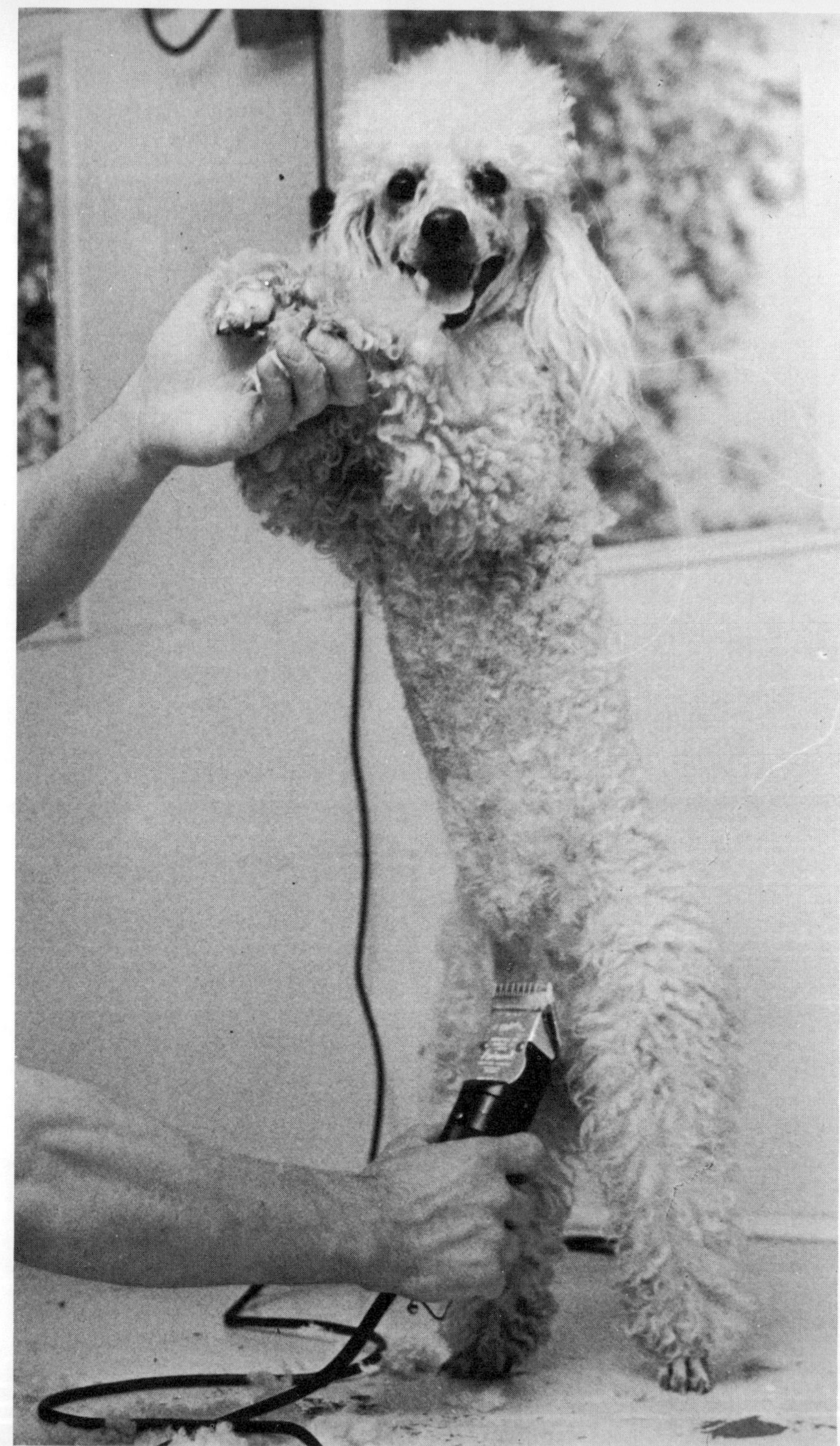

Even the pets need trimming

(Overleaf)
Two silver Pets

There are poodle clubs in many parts of the country, and you should have no difficulty in joining one within a reasonable distance of your home. They hold meetings, lectures, seminars, social functions and of course shows.

In addition you should subscribe to one of the dog papers so that you can keep in touch with the shows that are coming along in the near future. Unless you have already had some experience, it is as well to start with a smaller show and work your way gradually up to the bigger ones. As a novice, (if you are one), you will get kindly treatment at the smaller shows, but must

Discussing their grooming

(preceding page)
A group of Miniature Poodles at home

not expect any particular help from the judge and the officials at the big championship shows, where everyone starts equal. Most judges have a soft spot for a beginner, remembering that they themselves were once in a similar situation, but when things get serious and there is a great deal at stake it would be unfair to expect favours.

To gain experience, start with a variety show where all breeds can be

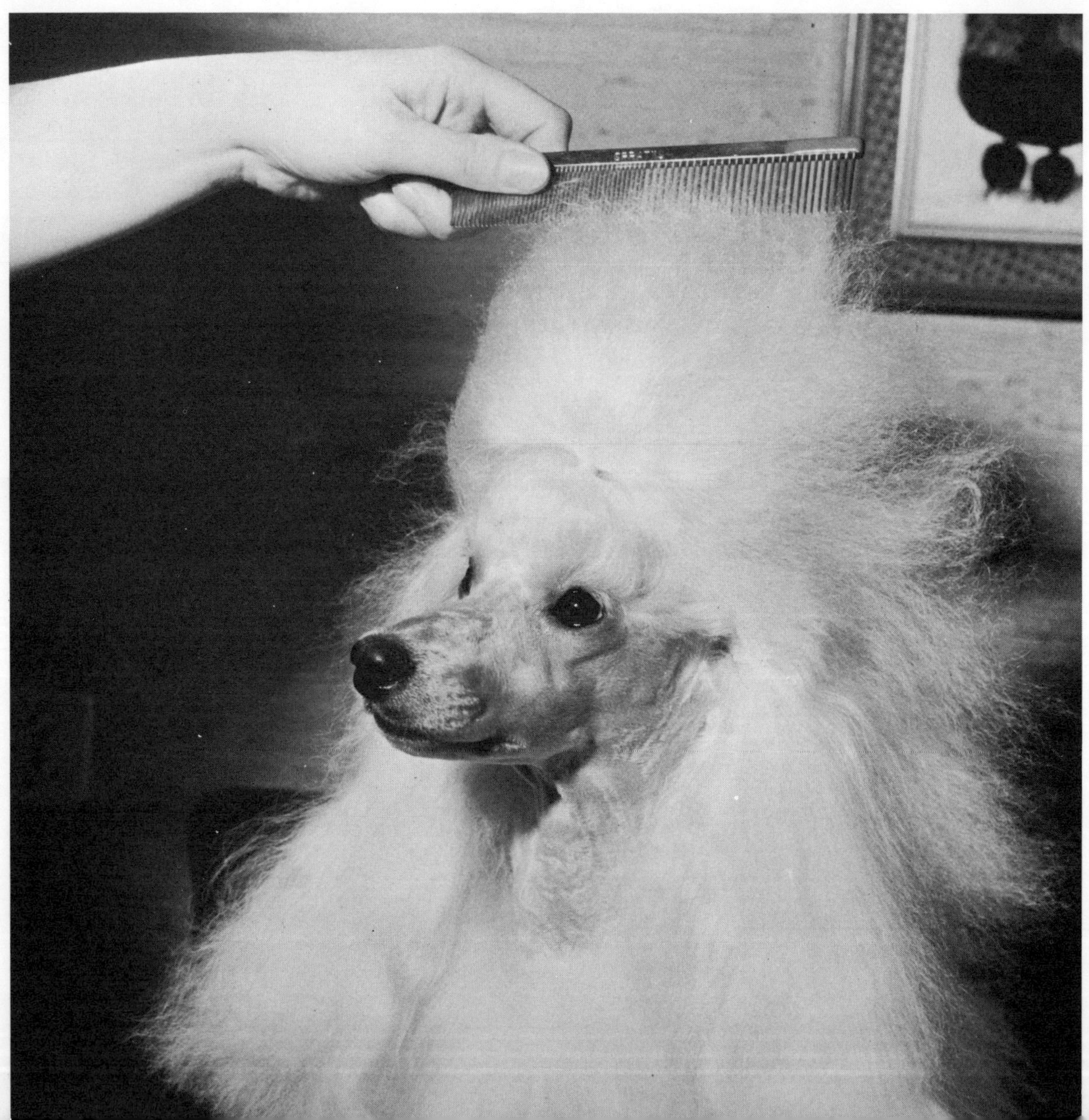

How the topknot is combed out

exhibited. It is best too to enter in the lowest possible class. Having seen the name and address in a dog paper, you write to the show secretary, and in return you receive a schedule of all the classes and all the information that you will need. You decide which class or classes you should enter your poodle in, and then send off your form and the entry fees.

From then on you should be concentrating on getting your poodle ready. You will have done all the preliminary clipping that is needed, but your dog still needs training. Showing a dog is not simply a question of walking into the ring with the poodle on the end of the lead and waiting for something to happen.

For many weeks before the show you should be training your poodle to stand correctly and to walk as the judge will want him to walk. Standing

Everything ready apart from the final touches

(opposite)
A white Standard at home

correctly only comes from constant training. He should stand with his head up and back, his tail held straight up, and his back legs stretched fairly well out behind him.

Constant practice is needed for this, and it can happily be combined with training your dog to move.

Moving consists of getting your poodle to trot at just the right speed for him, using all his legs correctly and evenly, with the legs at opposite corners moving forward at the same time. This can only be achieved by experiment.

Fantastic ear fringes grown by tying them up

Brushing right up to the last moment

The smaller your poodle, the slower you will need to walk; thus with a tiny Toy you will be walking quite slowly, whereas with a large adult Standard you will probably be running as fast as you can. It is as well to enlist the help of a friend, preferably someone with experience of dog showing, who will watch you move your dog and tell you to go faster or more slowly until you have got the correct speed fixed in your mind.

This can be coupled with standing practice. Ideally, every time that your poodle stops trotting he should immediately take up the correct stance. If you can manage this without getting down on your knees and propping him up, you will attract the judge's attention, as every judge prefers a dog to stand without being placed in position. So, having arrived at the correct speed for your poodle, you should for weeks before the show be taking him out for practice, moving him short distances and stopping constantly, encouraging him to move happily with his head and tail up, and to adopt the same stance whenever he stops. When he is wrong, correct him and start over again. Don't continue the exercise until he is completely bored. Once

Enormous coat on a tiny dog

(above)
Two that won the brace class at Crufts together

(above right)
Waiting for command

he is tired, break it off and rest, beginning again after a change or a suitable interval.

About three days before the show you should bath your poodle. Three days is about the minimum time for the coat to regain its natural oils and to cease being fluffy. You should then be constantly grooming right up to the show. This grooming stimulates the coat and restores its natural glow, so that by the time you enter the ring your poodle will be looking as near perfect as he can.

Once in the ring, grooming with brush and comb should cease. It is done by some people, but it must give spectators and judge the feeling that the

Champion Command Performance winning best in show at Westminster

dog was not properly prepared before it was taken into the ring. All that should now be needed is a gently stroking of the bulk of the hair over the back in a forward direction, in order to help it stay in position when the dog is standing. If the coat is of the correct texture, even this will not be needed.

All judges like a well-presented animal. Anything less will suggest that the exhibitor is not serious, and the animal will be penalised as a result. No dog repays time spent on its preparation more than a poodle does, and in no showring is the competition more keen. Your dog needs to enter the ring looking at his best, needs to be presented to the judge in the best possible way, and must be kept looking that way until the judge has finally made his decisions.

Ringcraft

Much has been written on the matter of how to exhibit a dog, but it will do no harm to reiterate some of the more important points.

If you are going to a show there are many more things that you need to know in addition to how to get your poodle ready: what to expect when you get there, what to take with you, and what to do to ensure that you are accepted by the other exhibitors and that you enjoy yourself.

One of the first lessons is to be a good loser. Poodles are very popular, not

Champion Petwill Nickelodian winning in America

only as pets, but in the showring, and you will almost certainly find yourself in competition with quite a large number of other exhibitors, many of whom – probably most – will have more experience than you. If you win any award at all, you should be very pleased; if you win first prize you have every reason for being delighted, and the other exhibitors will not grudge you your delight at victory. If you lose – and it must be remembered that if there are fifteen dogs in your class then eleven of them will get nothing – you will naturally be disappointed, but you should not be upset, just determined to persevere until you do better

If you start at a smaller show you will have none of the problems connected with 'benching', but will have others which can be just as troublesome. At an

What you get when you win

Miniature Poodle in Pet Clip

unbenched show you need to provide somewhere where your poodle can spend his time, somewhere away from the ring, where he can be comfortable, out of the way of other people and other dogs, and yet somewhere where you can attend to his coat and generally look after him. If he is small enough, then a portable dog box will do nicely; if he is too big for that, then you will need to provide a familiar rug or blanket on which he can sit.

You will also need all the grooming tools, combs, scissors and brushes that you normally use for his preparation. For these you need a container, preferably one that is specially made for the purpose with divisions for all the smaller articles and room for towels and larger pieces of equipment.

If the show is a benched one, then it is as well to arrive in good time to find your bench, set it up as you wish it to look with its rug and your equipment, and give the dog time to grow accustomed to what for him are completely strange surroundings.

Then find out which ring you are to show your dog in and make sure of the best route to it, avoiding as many other dogs and people as you possibly can. Next buy a catalogue and study it so that you can calculate when you and your dog will be required; your dog can then be perfectly groomed at just the right time. For getting to the ring on time is your problem. You will not normally be fetched, though the more kindly stewards will go to the trouble of doing this.

Once you are in the ring, try to discover what pattern the judge is using in his ring. Some will have one idea of how it should look: where the dogs that

Head of a Pet Poodle

Conversation piece between two Miniatures

he has not looked at should stand, in which direction they should move and where they should go to when he has finished looking at them. Others will have a different method. Unless you want to appear like a complete beginner, you should watch carefully what is going on, and follow the pattern without needing to be directed by the stewards who are in the ring with you.

When your class is over, unless you are in the following one, take your dog back to his bench and settle him down again. He has had a hard day – in fact, several hard days counting the time it has taken to get him ready – and he needs to relax.

It is as well not to feed your poodle before the show or during it, unless it is a very long show indeed. He will need water of course, several times during the day, and his water dish will be one of the things that you will need to take with you, but feeding is best left until you return home, when, after a long day, he will eat, take some exercise, and then enjoy a well-earned rest.

Feeding

There is nothing special about feeding poodles. The rules are the same, and the food is the same as for any other dog. There are as many diets as there are dogs, but the general principles are common throughout the whole of the canine race.

In their wild state, dogs are carnivores and the sort that hunt their own food rather than clean up after other animals, so that fresh raw meat is the natural food for the dog. But in the civilised world of today all forms of feeding have become more sophisticated, and it would be as wrong to feed

A silver Miniature Poodle in Dutch Clip

A Pet from Denmark

your poodle entirely on raw meat as it would be for you yourself to subsist entirely on nuts and berries.

Man has brought to bear a good deal of scientific knowledge on the matter of animal foodstuffs, and it is now possible to feed dogs quite successfully on compounded food in just the same way as poultry and cattle can be fed. Anyone who has owned a dog of any breed will have seen it eating grass. This was at one time thought to be a symptom of sickness and a desire on the part of the dog to get rid of something unwanted from its stomach. It is now known however that grass and greenery are essential to the wellbeing of the dog, and this habit was just his way of supplementing his diet with something that he needed.

Scientists have carefully analysed what mixture of carbohydrates, roughage, protein and minerals are needed for the complete food for dogs, and are now producing easily prepared food that satisfies a dog's every need.

In his early days as a puppy your poodle will need feeding on a 'little and often' pattern as would a baby animal of any species. As he grows older, the feeds become larger and the intervals longer, until as a mature animal most experts would recommend that he should have only one feed each day.

A Miniature in Puppy Clip

A black Miniature in traditional Lion Clip

The timing of this is important. In the wild state, a primitive dog would hunt, eat its food, and then rest in order to digest it. In our more civilised surroundings, with our dogs near, perhaps in our house and other people living all around us, we want our dogs to be as quiet as possible when we and other people are resting. Thus most breeders feed their dogs in the evening (sundown is a favourite time), so that they will settle down after their meal and possibly sleep through the night.

One of the things that can be troublesome with poodles is the fact that their ears are long and hang low down on their heads. This is a characteristic of the breed, and for show purposes the longer and lower they are the better. Unfortunately the ear fringes can fall into the food, and not only do they get soiled, but other dogs (if there are any) or even the poodle itself will chew the fringes as they taste good. There are several ways of keeping the ears out of the food, and the commonest is to fasten them up in some way.

If your poodle is a show dog, you will have the ear fringes permanently fastened up in pieces of material, plastic or similar held in place with rubber bands, which will keep the fringes away from the food bowl. If you do not wish to go to that trouble, the leg of an old sock passed over the head and ears

Called by some mismarks, by others harlequins

'Laying down the Law' by Sir Edwin Landseer, R.A.

will hold them back; but one of the best ways is to get your poodle into the habit of eating off a high place, a shelf or stool or even box, so that in reaching upwards the ears will fall back out of the bowl. Some exhibitors suggest that this also helps the poodle to improve its head carriage.

Finally, if after all this your poodle is any way unwell, don't try your own cures, don't ask advice from the man round the corner who knows about dogs, but get veterinary help immediately. When you have had him a while, your poodle will have become very precious to you, and you would not wish to run any more risks with his health than you would with your own.